Published by:
Gospel Standard Trust Publications

First printed :1997
Reprinted : 2003

ISBN 1-897837-08-9

Important Note

Comparing the accounts in the four Gospels, it is extremely difficult to be certain of the *exact* order of events, especially on the morning of the resurrection. One thing is clear. There must have been much coming and going of the godly women and the disciples, backwards and forwards, between the city of Jerusalem and the Lord's grave, and one house and another.

Printed in China by:

Hung Hing Off-set Printing Co., Ltd.

The Resurrection of Jesus

by

B.A.Ramsbottom

2003

Gospel Standard Trust Publications
12(b) Roundwood Lane
Harpenden, Hertfordshire
AL5 3DD, England

"Jesus is Alive"

It is very early in the morning and it is still dark. A few women are walking sadly through the streets of Jerusalem. Two of them are called Mary, another one Salome, and there are a few others with them as well.

Why are they looking so sad? Terrible things had been happening. They had seen the Lord Jesus crucified. He had been nailed to the cross. They had loved Him dearly – but now He was gone.

Now they were on their way to His grave. It was something like a cave, and a huge stone had been rolled in front of it. But they are worried. How can they move that great stone? They wanted to go inside to put sweet spices on the body of the Lord Jesus.

At last the women reached the garden where Jesus' grave was. But imagine their surprise! The stone was rolled away. Reverently they went inside – but there was no body there. What had happened? It seemed that someone must have stolen the body of Jesus, and taken it away.

They did not know that Jesus had come back to life. That was why His body was not there. During the night wonderful things had happened. A glorious angel had come down from heaven and rolled away the stone.

The soldiers, guarding the grave, had been terrified and ran away. The Lord Jesus, now alive, had left the grave.

But the women did not know this. All they could see was an empty grave. Poor Mary Magdalene was so distressed. Immediately she ran as fast as she could to tell the news to Peter and John. She knew they would be amazed to hear that the body of Jesus had disappeared. But while the other women wonder what to do, they see an angel in shining robes. He tells them something wonderful. Jesus is alive. They need not be frightened. They must go quickly and tell the disciples that He is risen from the dead. No wonder they ran as fast as they could with the good news.

But now Mary Magdalene has found Jesus' disciples, Peter and John. "They have taken the Lord away," she cries, "and we do not know where they have laid Him." She cannot think that Jesus is now alive – the wonderful truth: "THE LORD IS RISEN INDEED."

Of course, Peter and John are amazed. They hurry to the grave as quickly as they can – Mary following them.

John was the faster runner and got there first. He looked into the grave. How strange! No body – but the grave clothes neatly folded. When Peter arrived, he went straight in. And when John followed, it dawned on him immediately – Jesus is alive; that is why the grave is empty! What remarkable things the two of them had to talk about as they went back into the city!

How wonderful that Jesus is alive, never to die again!

You can read this story in Matthew chapter 28, verses 1 to 8, Mark chapter 16, verses 3 to 7, and John chapter 20, verses 1 to 10.

The first Christians used to greet each other on the Lord's day morning with "THE LORD IS RISEN INDEED."

Mary Magdalene

See this sorrowful woman standing by the grave of Jesus. She is crying bitterly. Yes, it is Mary Magdalene. She has come back to the grave after Peter and John have gone. She cannot keep away.

Mary had been a very wicked woman. But Jesus had forgiven all her sins. She very dearly loved the Lord Jesus for all that He had done for her. She could not bear to think of the cruel death He died on the cross. Now even His body was gone. She was not there when the angel told the other women that He was risen.

She was sad because she had lost her dearest friend. But other things made her sad. Had not Jesus said He was the Son of God? But now He is dead.... What of her sins?

However, she thought she would have another look inside the grave. And two angels were there! One was sitting where Jesus' head had been, and the other where Jesus' feet had been. They asked her why she was crying. It seemed a foolish question to Mary. Surely everyone knew why she was crying. "They have taken away my Lord, and I know not where they have laid Him."

She turned sadly away from the grave. Someone was standing there in the garden – a Stranger. And the

Stranger asked her just the same question as the angels: why was she crying?

You know who this Stranger was, don't you? It was Jesus, just risen from the dead. But Mary Magdalene did not know. She thought He was only the gardener. So she asked Him if He was the one who had taken the body away. Perhaps she did not really look, or her eyes were filled with tears.

Then she heard the sweetest sound she had ever heard in her life. It was the voice of Jesus. He was speaking her name. He was saying, "Mary." It was only one word, but it meant everything to Mary Magdalene. Her Lord and Master was alive. He *was* the Son of God. He did still love her. "Fear not, I have redeemed thee; I have called thee by thy name; thou art Mine."

Quickly Mary replied, "Rabboni!" – my dearest Lord and Master. She worshipped Him.

Then Jesus said a strange thing to her: "Do not touch Me." (Later He *told* the disciples to touch Him.) It seems that Mary thought everything was going to go on just as before. She wanted to cling to Him. But Jesus told her that He was not going to stay on earth for long. He was going back to heaven to His Father – "your Father," he told Mary. And she was to go and tell the disciples all that had happened.

What a meeting it must have been when Mary came

to the disciples and told them all the wonderful things that had happened! She had seen the Lord, no longer dead but alive again, and He had talked with her.

You can read about this in John chapter 20, verses 11 to 18.

We keep Sunday as the Sabbath, the Lord's day, because Jesus rose from the dead "early on the first day of the week."

Jesus' Second Appearance

Now what had happened to the other women? Can you remember, they had seen an angel? He had told them Jesus was alive. Now they were hurrying to tell the good news to the disciples. They ran as quickly as they could. What strange feelings they had – so happy, because of what they had heard; still afraid, because of what they had seen!

Suddenly, as they hurry along the road into Jerusalem, someone is coming to meet them. Can it be true? Yes, it is Jesus Himself. Lovingly He greets them. He says, "All hail!"

We do not read they spoke a single word. But together they all fell down at His feet. Tenderly they held those feet that on the Friday before had been pierced by the cruel nails. They worshipped Him. Their hearts were full of love and joy and thankfulness. Their Lord and Master was with them once again.

Jesus spoke very kindly to them. He told them not to be frightened; there was nothing to be frightened of, though they had been shaking with fear. They must take a message to the disciples – He kindly calls them, "My brethren." The disciples must go back to Galilee, and they will see Him there.

This was the *second* time Jesus appeared. He was

to stay on earth for forty days, and then go back to heaven to His Father. But *all* His disciples would see Him, and some more of His friends. So many would be able to say, "We have seen the Lord" – though at first some could hardly believe it was true.

You can read about this in Matthew chapter 28, verses 9 and 10.

We must only worship God. But have you noticed, when people worshipped the Lord Jesus, He did not forbid them?

The Emmaus Road

It was a spring day, the day Jesus rose from the dead. Two of His followers were going on a long journey to a place called Emmaus. The countryside must have been lovely, but both of them were sad.

As they went along, they talked earnestly together. They could not understand what had happened. They were followers of Jesus and hoped He would be a great leader who would set His people free. Now He was dead.... But then some people said He was alive again.... They were just bewildered.

But who is this joining them? Jesus Himself. He journeyed along with them – but they did not know it was Jesus. Again and again when people saw Jesus after He rose again, they did not recognise Him, did they?

Then Jesus asked them a question. "What are you talking about?" They were amazed. Was not everybody talking about the same thing? Who was this Stranger? And why had He not heard? They asked Him if He was just a visitor as He did not seem to know about all these things that had happened in Jerusalem.

So Jesus asked them, "What things?" He knew, of course, but He wanted to listen to what they had to say. What a tale of sadness it was! What they had hoped of

this Jesus, and how they were disappointed. And Jesus quietly listened to all they had to say. How wonderful that Jesus, now in heaven, still listens when His people tell Him their troubles! He is so kind and gracious.

And then at last Jesus began to speak. He preached a sermon to them about Himself. It must have been the most wonderful sermon ever preached – and there were only two listening to it.

They were amazed. He told them that they should not have been surprised that their Lord and Master had died. He came on purpose to die for His people – to save them from their sins, not to set them free from the Roman Emperor. The Old Testament Bible said all this. And also He came to rise again – they should not be surprised to hear rumours of this!

Still they do not know who He is, but in no time they reach Emmaus, the place where they were going. But no! He seems as if He is going to leave them. They beg Him to stay with them. They say, "Abide with us." Do you know the well-known hymn:

"Abide with me, fast falls the eventide,
  The darkness deepens; Lord, with me abide"?

Kindly He did what they asked Him. Then suddenly, as they were eating and drinking together, they realised who He was, the Lord Jesus Himself. And then He disappeared.

What thoughts they must have had! Yes, Jesus was alive. But why had they not realised it was Jesus? They could not help thinking of how happy they had been listening to Him on their long walk. Their hearts had felt warm.

And then, what do you think they did? They got straight up, and walked back all the way to Jerusalem. They had just been walking for about two hours, and it would take another two hours for them to get back; but they longed to tell the disciples the good news. What things they must have talked about on the way!

When they found the disciples, Peter had already met the living Jesus and told them Jesus was alive. But the two were able to say, "Yes, we know it is true. We have seen Him ourselves."

You can read about this in Luke chapter 24, verses 13 to 35.

Jesus still listens when we pray, when we confess our sins, and when we tell Him our troubles.

Easter Evening

It was the evening of the day when Jesus rose from the dead. It had been a wonderful day. Such remarkable things had been happening. The disciples were met all together, no doubt in the upper room where He had talked with them before He was crucified.

But there were only ten of them. Judas Iscariot, the traitor, was now dead. Another disciple, Thomas, was also missing. It seems he thought there was no point in their meeting together if their Saviour was no longer with them. And now they had just been joined by the two from Emmaus with their exciting news. But the little group securely fastened the doors so that no one could get in. They were frightened. You can guess why. His enemies had killed their Lord; perhaps they would try to kill them.

But who is this? In a moment, there is the Lord Jesus standing among them. No doors can keep Him out. But they were terrified. They thought it must be a ghost.

Jesus spoke so kindly to them. He said, "Peace be unto you." And then He did an amazing thing. He showed them His hands and His feet – where the cruel nails had wounded Him. How sad they must have been

looking on His wounds, remembering how He died on the cross, but how glad to know it really was the Lord Jesus, and that He was alive! What must they have thought? Those wounds were the marks of His love when He died for them. Was there ever love like that of Jesus?

He even told His disciples to take hold of Him – to show that He was a real Man, not some kind of spirit. And then He ate a piece of fish and some honey; no ghost can do that! No wonder they were so happy.

Before leaving them, the Lord Jesus spoke to them about Himself, teaching them from the Bible. Have you noticed how dearly Jesus loved the Bible, the Word of God? He told them that they too would have to be teachers, telling people that only the risen Jesus could forgive sin, and that He would forgive all whom the Holy Spirit made truly sorry. One thing they would be able to teach clearly – that Jesus died and rose again. They knew that.

You can read about this in Luke chapter 24, verses 36 to 48 and John chapter 20, verses 19 and 20.

Jesus loved the Bible and tells us, "Search the Scriptures." Do you read the Bible?

Thomas

But what about Thomas? Of course, the disciples told him what had happened, that Jesus was alive. But Thomas just did not believe them. It seemed ridiculous. How can anyone who is dead come back to life?

Poor Thomas! We call him "doubting Thomas," don't we? He even said he would *not* believe unless he not only saw Jesus, but was allowed to put his finger where the nails had cut Jesus' hands, and put his hand in the wound the spear had made in Jesus' side. Thomas needed a lot to make *him* believe.

A week later once again the disciples are met together – this time eleven of them. Yes, Thomas is there. I wonder why he came? Could he not keep away? Again the doors are tightly shut. Again Jesus stands among them.

Then He turns to Thomas. Whatever will He say to him? Listen, He tells Thomas to put his fingers where the nails had been, and to put his hand in the wound in His side – the very words that Thomas had used the week before. How did Jesus know? Did you know He is the unseen listener to every conversation? He hears everything we say. Now He tells Thomas "not to be faithless but believing."

I don't think Thomas did put his fingers in the nail

prints, do you? Or his hand in Jesus' wounded side?
Full of shame for what he had said, and full of love to
the risen Saviour, he fell at His feet and worshipped
Him. He cried, "My Lord and my God."

And Jesus was not displeased because Thomas
called Him God. That is who He is – true, almighty
God, the One who made all things.

*You can read about this in John chapter 20, verses
24 to 29.*

The Disciples of the Lord

A few days after this Peter decided to go back to his fishing. After all, now Jesus was not with them all the time, what else could he do? So "I go a-fishing," he cried. There were six other disciples with him. "We will go too," they said.

Well, they did not do very well with their fishing. They were out on the lake all night, but they did not catch one single fish. They must have been very disappointed – and tired.

Next morning, as they were sailing back to the shore, they could see someone standing there. It was Jesus – but once again His followers could not recognise Him.

When they were near enough to hear His voice, the Stranger called to them. Had they any fish? "No," they said – not very kindly, it seems.

Then the Stranger told them to do something. "Throw the fishing net on the other side of the ship." But why? Peter was a skilful fisherman. He knew the lake well. What hope of catching any fish in the morning after such a night? Yet he did as he was told. Was there an unseen power in the words of Jesus? "Never man spake like this Man."

But what is happening? A multitude of fish, so many that the disciples cannot pull them all in. A miracle!

Suddenly John realises. "It is the Lord!" he cries in wonder and love. And before we know what is happening Peter is over the side of the boat swimming to shore. How Peter loved Jesus! He could not get there quickly enough. He could not wait for the boat to take him there.

The other disciples followed, dragging the net full of fishes – 153 altogether. Was Peter not bothered about the fish any more?

And there the Lord Jesus had already lit a fire to warm them, and was cooking fish for them to eat – for they must have been hungry. The kindness of Jesus is very wonderful. "Come and dine!" He said. And what a meal it must have been!

You can read about this in John chapter 21, verses 1 to 14.

Jesus and Peter

Soon the meal was ended. Will Jesus leave them now – as He had done before? Usually, after His resurrection, He did not stay with them long.

But no! He is talking to Peter. What is He saying? Three times He asks him if he really loves Him. "Lovest thou Me?"

Do you remember what Peter had done just before Jesus was put to death? Three times he had said that he did not even know Him. He had sinned badly. He had denied his Lord and Master. Then a cock crowed – and Peter remembered Jesus had warned him, and he went out and cried bitterly. He was deeply sad because of what he had done.

In love and mercy Jesus had forgiven him. But had he said three times that he did not even know Jesus? Then three times he must answer the question whether he truly did love the Lord. And each time he said, Yes. The last time, being sad that Jesus again asked him the same question, he added: "Lord, Thou knowest all things. Thou knowest that I love Thee."

Yes, Peter did love Jesus, despite what he had done. He loved Jesus very dearly. It is a wonderful thing if we truly love the Lord Jesus.

Then Jesus told him, "Feed My lambs. Feed My

sheep." No, Jesus had not cast him away as a disciple. The rest of his life is to be spent preaching – not going back to his old life as a fisherman! He is to tell sinners all about his Lord and Master – who He is, what He has done, that He died and rose again – that He saves His people from their sins.

Later in the Bible we read of how Peter preached, and how the Lord blessed him, especially on the Day of Pentecost. Again, he spoke wonderful words about the name of Jesus: "There is none other name whereby we must be saved." Do you know the hymn, "How sweet the name of Jesus sounds"?

Peter must serve Jesus right to the end, even till he died. And Jesus told him that at last he would be put to death because he was one of His followers.

"Follow Me!" He said to Peter – and so He still speaks to His people now.

You can read about this in John chapter 21, verses 15 to 23.

"Hark, my soul! it is the Lord;
 'Tis thy Saviour, hear His Word;
 Jesus speaks, and speaks to thee:
 'Say, poor sinner, lovest thou Me?'"

The Gathering on the Mountain

Have you ever climbed a mountain? Often it is very beautiful, but sometimes very rough and rugged. Usually mountains are lonely places; there are few people about.

But this mountain is not lonely. Crowds of people are climbing it. I wonder why? We do not know the name of the mountain, but it is a mountain in Galilee, where Jesus had lived. He has promised that He will meet His followers and friends on this mountain on a certain day. That is why they are all coming.

You can imagine how excited they were when the day came, and as they gathered together. They longed to see the risen Saviour. We are told that more than five hundred were there altogether.

We cannot help wondering who those five hundred were? Was one the poor leper Jesus made better? Was another one Lazarus, whom Jesus raised from the dead? Was Zacchaeus there? What about blind Bartimaeus? We are sure Mary and Martha would have been present if they could. We wonder if Mary the Mother of Jesus managed to get there, to see her Son. The disciples would be there – but not Judas Iscariot. What about the woman at the well? What about Nicodemus?

We do not know. But was there ever such a

gathering? And at last Jesus appeared. They were not disappointed. With delight they looked on Him, the risen Saviour. And He had some wonderful things to say. He promised that, though they would not be able to see Him, He would always be with them, even to the end of the world.

Years later, when Paul was writing about Jesus rising from the dead, most of the five hundred were still alive.

What a wonderful gathering that will be when all God's people gather together to meet their Lord and Saviour in heaven! The important question is: "Will you be there?"

You can read about this in 1 Corinthians chapter 15, verse 6. (Probably Matthew chapter 28, verses 16 to 20, speaks of the same time.)

The Ascension

Those must have been wonderful days when the risen Saviour, the Lord Jesus, met with His disciples again and again and kindly talked with them. But they were not going to last for ever. Jesus must go back to His Father in heaven.

It was now forty days (over a month) since Jesus rose from the dead. One day He took His disciples for a walk. They were going to Bethany. They had to go across the Mount of Olives. How lovely everything must have seemed in the beautiful springtime, but especially how lovely to walk with Jesus by their side!

Suddenly Jesus stopped. He raised His hands. He blessed them. But what is happening now? Jesus is rising from the earth. He is moving up into the air. Higher and higher He goes. They stand there, watching. There He is passing into the sky. At last He is out of their sight, hidden behind a cloud.

You can imagine what they all did. They just stood there, amazed, gazing up into the sky. What had happened? Where had Jesus gone? What should they do?

But all at once two angels in shining white robes appear. They stand by them. They speak to them. What are they saying? That Jesus has gone back to

heaven. But one day He will come back from heaven to earth. He will not come as a baby as He did to Bethlehem. He will come in great power and glory with all His holy angels with Him. There will be a shout. There will be the sound of a trumpet. Jesus will come again as a Judge, as an Almighty King. Till then He lives and reigns in heaven.

The important thing is to be ready for when Jesus comes again, a true believer on Him the Son of God, washed in His blood, made ready for heaven. How solemn not to be ready! How blessed to be prepared for His coming!

May we each pray to know the risen Saviour for ourselves that when He does come again, we might each be prepared, made ready by God's grace.

You can read about this in Luke chapter 24, verses 50 to 52 and Acts chapter 1, verses 9 to 11.

A good prayer: "Lord Jesus, forgive me. Wash away my sins. Make me right. May I be ready when Thou dost come again."